MW00964210

SOMETHING BURNED ALONG
THE SOUTHERN BORDER

Copyright © Robert Earl Stewart 2009
All rights reserved
Printed in Canada

Library and Archives Canada Cataloguing in Publication

Stewart, Robert Earl, 1974-
Something burned along the southern border / Robert
Earl Stewart.

Poems.
ISBN 978-1-894469-44-9

I. Title.

PS8637.T4955S65 2009   C811'.6   C2009-905212-1

Editor for the Press: Stuart Ross
Cover Design: Mansfield Creative
Author Photo: Robert Earl Stewart
Typesetting: Stuart Ross

The publication of *Something Burned Along the Southern Border*
has been generously supported by
The Canada Council for the Arts and
The Ontario Arts Council.

 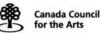

Mansfield Press Inc.
25 Mansfield Avenue, Toronto, Ontario, Canada M6J 2A9
Publisher: Denis De Klerck
www.mansfieldpress.net

for my mother,
Bethia Caldwell Stewart
(1948–2006)

CONTENTS

Father, why does this night
last longer than any other night?

For God is not a secret.

— David Berman
   "Now II"

I

FIELD NOTES TOWARDS A DEEPER UNDERSTANDING

The moon was like the residue of sale-price sticker peeled from a pale blue
album cover—and I was the first delicate creature of the spring.

The broken cookies fell from the blue monster's mouth, uneaten—
and this was the first hard lesson about puppetry.

Mrs. Randma's wig rolled like a wheel seeking a shave beneath the speeding
fire engine as we stood apple-cheeked in the fall wind—
this was when "embarrassment" first entered our vocabulary.

A half-eaten Caramilk tucked in my report card and tossed out the window
of my grandfather's Omni northbound on Campbell Street—
and I learned that a misguided gesture can have unintended effects.

It was the day—no, the hour—of ripeness ...
and we filled plastic grocery bags with peaches from Mr. Hickey's tree.
Wasps did not swarm around our ankles or heads because not one peach
had fallen to rot in the tall grass, but I barely made the bike ride home
from eating too many in the picking—
and perfection became a liquor too sickly sweet.

The girl who asked me to the prom and left the party in tears, intact—
it was possible, I saw, to be too much the gentleman.

I dreamt I was fitting small songbirds with suits
of custom-designed armour—and learned not to spend the moments
before a nap studying *Sibley's Field Guide to Birds of Eastern North America*.

I didn't burn out my arm throwing curveballs because I was not allowed
to throw one. I burnt everything else out though,
in a big dark somnolence of the soul—the last lasting lesson at the bottom.

I was the first delicate creature of the spring. I was stalked by wolves,
followed by bears, and flushed from hiding like a deer
by an inebriate tribe and their quiet "Darts" incantation
and the realization upon waking
that I have a responsibility to the night.

PRESENTING THE SLEEP OF DOLLS

The Sleep of Dolls is a series of eight photographs
shot in secret in my parents' home.
In them, a doll, Cookie, stands among orchids,

stares from windows into a nondescript spring,
understands time, its uncertainty,
and her uncertain place in it.

She spends uncertain minutes before a mirror.
She falls into meaningless sleep
across the foot of my parents' bed—

the sleep is the sleep of dolls:

hinged eyes louvred shut,
lips bowed like the arc of a bad story,
a melodrama about a naughty doll
who turned to drink

when she came to know too much about herself,
about her waking sleep, the way mechanism
creaked inside her like a clock.

You should know some things about Cookie: she belonged
to my grandmother and came from Scotland.
There are photos of me sitting with her, repaired club foot
in a cast of old-school white plaster. Her demeanour
that of a ghost caught in resin—

she stares off into that Oshawa apartment with 1975's ennui—
a look she will affect over the next thirty years,
until the moment I pull her from the closet
and pose her by a bowl of white orchids.

I have been warned this could shatter
happy childhood memories—
times before the doll hospital reparations, before I knew
she was lonely and aware.

But with my camera, I was merely there the way flowers
are there, the way the clock or the bottle is there.

Like the unchallenged pane of glass.
Uninvited, like the clouds.

ANALOG

The suspicion that I was like something
kept pace with me
and one day I realized what it was:
I had become like the small sponge robot—
a toy on the insipid cusp—
my cousin and I put in the bathtub
in direct contravention of the instructions
on the package.

I REMEMBER THE WAY THINGS WEREN'T

for Mike M.

One of the last people I ever got drunk with
claimed to have invented a laser—
the laser—
that would revolutionize
the cult of the precision tool.

"Suzanne,"
he would say to his ex-wife, "I may not remember the way things were,
but I sure as hell remember the way things weren't."

I went around, repeating this line for a long time,
like a joke,

oblivious as to how his cold hardwood home,
blaring Charles Ives and King Crimson,
nothing around but a baby grand and a bag of chocolate in the fridge,
was connected to my own—

there must've been a door,
bevelled into the newels, or fading into
the wainscoting, through a series of pantries,
broom closets, wallpapered domestic channels,
kitchens of nondescript failure—
oblivious, in the labyrinth of my disease,

that there was no such device,
that my belief was as fucked as his delusion,

that I wasn't remembering the way things were, either,

and remembering how they weren't
is a waking dream.

Try looking at a clock, turning on the lights.

KITES ARE VERY POPULAR THIS YEAR,
BY THE LOOKS OF THE PARK

I was back in the school last night,
scouting the set for the penultimate scene

in a novel I alternately write, revile,
        and dream. The continued hush

past the initial quietening down—
        like crumbs in the thread count of sleep—

        is impossibly human, a somnambulist
disappearing in the landscape of deoxygenated

blood in the time between first light
        and the alarm.

        We could go to war with the clouds
today. Instead we enjoy the tug on us—

the flag flap and that tug,
        as familiar as the jiggle at depth

        when something strikes the line;
when the archetypes of fear

become trouble in dreams; a plague
        drinking Marco Petri on the avenue,

tipping into the waking life,
        hugging the pitiful earth: languid, shamed

by the inability
        to understand the wind, the tautness

of the string unseen, the privilege of truce
　　　　with gravity, the transcendence of the windsock's

deep bowl, looking down through eyes drawn
　　　　on the backs of hands at the candy coat

of ground glass; the flare as the unseen hand
　　　　of gentle detonation touches its fingers to the wick;

the sudden presence of shrikes—they overwhelm the darkness
　　　　with the coding and deciphering of messages dispatched

and delivered by pigeons, whose horrible wingbeats
　　　　drown out the sound of the original engines of fear,

　　　　the gang-related comedy of the fatal metalmarks, and
the compositional hallmarks of sleep paralysis.

　　　　I liked it better when I mistook this failure
as something else, like pantomime.

THE VISCOUNT HOTEL

We agree that Kubrick went out like a man,
with all the bush at that *Eyes Wide Shut* party.

We assume that the secret to the secret handshake
is avoiding the secret handshake,

like loathsome jazz concepts perpetrated by some bachelor
of philosophy, who swaggers like the history of black music is springing
from a well in his doll-smooth forehead.

You confess that as a youth, you would urinate heartily
into the rooftop pool, when your family went swimming
at the Viscount Hotel.

I accept your confession in my official capacity
as Prelate of the Curio of Moy Avenue,
and subject you to a retelling of an awkward
hour from my formative moments:

I scrawl "FUCK" in the talcum powder dust
on the lid of my mother's jewellery box,
all rosewood and negative space,
gleaming fingertip polish hemmed in by dull fields.
The terminus of each stroke
the whorl of my offending finger;

the word trebled, like a match flame
held at the base of the vanity mirror;
like the top half of a little "FUCK" sandwich,
ready to be flipped down on a quicksilver hinge.

When my mother discovers
my communiqué, I have to dust it off
through a plague of embarrassment that lasts forever.

Because nothing else is said about "FUCK"—
either because these things happen
or because we didn't swear in our house—
and I had jumped all the way to the worst-case scenario

for my first public language experiment at ten, daring
the Vienna School to hop the next flight to here
and smoke cigars with me, examine scars with me,
exchange secret handshakes.

CINÉMA DU PARC

I laugh all the way
through *The Garden of the Finzi-Continis*
during Passover in the second row at Cinéma du Parc.

Entering the men's room—
red smears for eyes and mellowed to the point of having kittens—
I found a Japanese woman in her house shirt
washing her hands at the sink, speaking at me
through the mirror, losing me utterly,
and not just because of the hand dryer's roar, but because
she insisted on speaking Japanese.
I replied with a shouted "Is this the men's room?" before disappearing
into a stall and ghost urinating while planning my escape
through the crowded lobby.

People come to visit me. Drinks are served.
My studio apartment in the Ghetto is hotboxed beyond its dimensions.
We walk from there to see *The Exorcist* (one midnight only)
and are met at the top of 1972's award winner for
Achievement in Surreal Staircases and Cantilevered Galleries
by a double-helix tendril of exploded starch, a wick
of hot grease, and *la securité*.

The movie was too evil for the venue:
the eccentric seats and giant hairs jerking
in the grain of the screen, the tubular pop of the sound system,
the stoners counting breaths in the flicker.

Covered in hickory sticks
after a first-row snoring clinic brought on
by an afternoon at the Peel Pub on the
Red Cross tab, I high-step out of *Brazil*
and have an as-of-yet unfinished jeremiad addressed
to Terry Gilliam buried in the walls of 3450 Durocher #4
where I no longer live.

And then, one night post-Halloween,
after seeing *L.A. Confidential*—
three empties left neatly in the aisle at my ramshackle seat—
on Milton beneath a parked car

I find a cache of another man's photos.

PERSPECTIVES ON THE DEATH OF AN AMATEUR FILMMAKER

i.

Mr. Chocolate found the note in the maze.
Impaled on a branch, it was her brassiere.
He carried it back to the other bears;
they knew they had to honour his request
at least in principle: an end had come
to their détente. Evidence suppression
was not a specialty of the ursans.
Some bear from the interior would come.
The man knew nothing about drought; nothing
about predation and intrusion; spoke
to them the way most people speak to pets—
as a special character they perform
in private. They should've killed him the day
he first strolled onto the mudflats and spoke.

ii.

Dear Field Journal: I've left
the bears some of her things. I've done the
one thing I said I'd never ask of them.
In the airport she said she's now afraid—
that she's going to leave me before the end
of the season. The pilot knows she's here,
but I can lure him to shore when he comes
to fly us out. The camera will be off.
They will know what a full-blooded hombre
I am. I've become so tight with them I can
make them do this; I'm not afraid to ask.
I'm not afraid to kill the bush pilot.
I'm a filmmaker. I'm a bear lover.
No one will ever leave me on their terms.

iii.

When I watch the movie, I hear myself
telling Werner about his spine, his watch—
but all I see are the flies on my skin,
in my mouth, eyes ... and I'm alive. I can't
imagine what it would be like for them,
unable to get away from the flies.
They've never bugged me before. I hate them
now. I might change jobs. Get out of flying.
Maybe work with kids, flowers, but not bears.
When I watch the movie and see myself
landing the plane, helping him and the girl
unload that one last time, I can't help but
wonder: could I have stopped them so late in
the season? Then I hear the flies.

AN HOSTILITY OF TOYS

And finally, eventually,
you arrive at this place, this station in life,
where the only strain of control you have
is an angry brand of housework:
the dishes as a form of judgment,
free-range paper detail as criticism,
where she leaves things as psychoanalysis,
laundry as theatre—
and then you have children. And then everything
becomes a kind of porn:
sterilization, the expected domestic ideal;
a fetish of folding in a vacuum of sleep, where no
stolen moments escape, kisses go unbestowed
in favour of another pass with the vacuum,
no sweet gesture goes unpunished. And you are naught.
The house is lost.

A group of turkeys is a raft; crows a murder.
Priests come in a blackness; a consumption of pies;
a mullet of wankers; an equivocation of Jesuits;
a transcendence of marijuana; an insolvency
of arts majors—
and this second carpet of children's things,
when I walk in the door and see it now,
this hostility of toys, I know it is a blessing.
Where would I be if this was suddenly taken from us?
Give over your need to alphabetize and cubbyhole
along with your need to drive a stake
through the heart of disarray, and instead drive
it through the heart of order, and raise a flag on it,
a standard above your fortress of couch cushions and afghans,
where you read comics and eat grapes and cheese
and spend whole evenings on your knees,
and live here, unapologetically.

NOTICE TO MARINERS

The vessel of your love is matchsticks.
You're taking on water in secret.
You're listening to separate radios in private.
You're guided by voices neither has charted in the other.
And a ten-minute how-to restoration film
is dirty footage of a mistress—
the smallest, most savage
mistress with opposable thumbs,
capable of leveraging tools in times of war.

Capsized and gone, your friends had it made.
You cried for them for a season, not realizing you cried
for the gulf being carved by unseen streams between you.
They died holding each other in the last available air
in the roof of their hull.

While every tack you execute takes you further
from each other, your familiar infatuations,
until you are foundering by compass and sextant,
aligned to the club and its abortive mission.

FUSELAGE, MANITOBA

That there were more wrecked planes around than bears
was a fact not lost on them. They wrote to their wives
to advise they would be squatting
on Crown Land in a nose cone (*send liquor*).
The closest dwellings had boards hammered through
with nails covering every orifice. The wildflowers
below the windows were often bent with black gore,
and even some bright red.
When they asked the guide if skeletons were
ever found in the wrecks that speckled the
terrain like different-coloured pins,
he said: "Bears take care of that."
Airplane steel gaping like a foil chip bag—
windows and hatches flung or disappeared,
giving up secrets of luggage evolution,
presenting a spread of plush seats,
major traumatic flaws shiny after the rain;
occasionally, wings and tails.
They decided they'd rather risk emaciated bears—
one's giving up a lucrative practice in sedation dentistry;
the other a lucrative career in insurance fraud—
than fall prey to the dispersal
pattern of grounded bait in a self-fulfilling
treeline economy (*send adult things*).
A poll of their friends would've revealed: 1)
neither was known as a photographer;
and 2) they would be picked clean (*send regards*).

THE CIRCUITOUS ROUTE TO LIMA

Should I ever come down with Capgras
delusion like a fever on the way home
from work one night

convince me, imposter wife,
that not only are you the illusory double,
but my kidnapper as well,

an idealist holding me for ransom
for your cause,

and I will fall in love with you
all over again

because I have Stockholm
syndrome, too,

and your cause is that
people take me seriously.

LOVE, PINEAPPLE

I'm chopping pineapples at dusk, alone.
Alone. Chopping. Dusk. Pineapples. A knife.
Pineapples falling to pieces in the night.
In the twilight, a knife, chopping.
I'm alone. So desperately alone with this fucking pineapple.
Chopping, chopping, chopping—a little dicing in the dusk—
and putting bits of pineapple in a bowl:
a lonely little bowl of nighttime pineapple.
I'm knifing this thing to nighttime.
I'm dusky and chopped up in this bowl of loneliness.
I'm lonely and covered in pineapple juice,
chopping up the twilight into digestible fruit-salad–sized choppings.
At dusk. My God, this pineapple.
My God, my knife so lonely.

SIDNEY CROSBY

She was younger than my most recent
memory of a soft drink.
She told me she wasn't even remotely

interested in band—
she just liked roller coasters and boys,
in that order.

When she met someone new,
she would latch on to some macabre
personal detail

and it would crop up in her conversation,
a sounding for a depth
she wasn't sure was there;

unsure herself whether she was mocking,
or pitying, or both; turning it over
like a mysterious old chestnut:

"The day I met her was her birthday," she'd say,
"and she had to go feed her grandmother."

She worried she would find and fall in love
with a boy who would need the birds
and the bees explained to him

with those dolls they keep at the police station.
She worried Sidney Crosby
might be that boy.

"I would never stop being honoured,"
she said, when I told her about this poem.

"Is it illegal for you to take what I say
and reproduce it without my knowledge?" she asked.

"Probably," I said.
She sulked for a bit, then said:

"Do you still want to work behind the meat counter
at Schwab's? I just love the image of you in a paper hat."

And just like that,
she had me where she wanted me.
I put down my pen.

NIGHT'S RUST

In my loneliness I slept deeply.
The room had a mirror whose edges were giving
way to a darkness like something burned
along its southern border. As I slept
I felt that heat transfer through the Travelodge
and start at my feet beneath the floral
print, transferring that nacreous background
brown of the black gold of mirror backs
like a consumption, eating like night's rust.

In the morning I'm right up close—mental
like the craftsmen with the arctic spar—
leaving ghosts of bathymetric fog there.
And I cannot touch the mirror, only the ghost-
making glass. Then there's a space before the silver.

WOLVES

Those coyotes you see grinning in the gravel
are not German shepherds.
The German shepherds that slink along the easements
and baste poultry alive with their satanic eyes and rotisserie
brains are not coyotes.

Those hackled ribbed things,
unfurling themselves into the night, haunted houses
born behind the teeth and shot through with luna:

We are the Wolves of Essex County.
We act like coyotes, we outnumber German shepherds,
we have our eyes on your women.

You can see the woodlots where they've been pushed,
like hale welterweights into thicket corners,
from every road outside the city limits.
Stands of maple, oak, ash, sumac, chestnut, willow,
Kentucky coffee and impenetrable deadfall and ground cover, lush,

dark and untouched domes on the sacred back acreage
of every farm. Know that their density is lupine—
the surface tension of foliage, if broken,
would peel away to a nightmare of pelts, a pack
in the deepest, cruelest sense of the word—

stacked wolf against wolf against tree
against abandoned combine against wolf,
no room for the young, let alone the modern conveniences.

So it is that someone is voted to follow the CN tracks into town,
to exact some revenge
for what the county forester says is an army ten thousand strong,
ghettoized on less than one per cent of the land.

When we were young, one found its way into Willistead Park
where it was brought down by standard-issue WPD ammo
after a brief stand-off. There was no note.
The wolves did not issue a statement.

In fact, it was reported that it was not a wolf at all,
but a coyote—fool enough to come back to the city.

For that, it was decapitated and tested for the fear of water
and its cameo petered out in the briefs section
on the fifth day,
no one bothering to report that it wasn't a coyote at all,
but an emissary from the wolves.

Then the other morning, a woman in Old Walkerville awoke
to a sound outside her bedroom.

She crept from bed and opened the door,
encountering a shirtless man
in khaki pants and a painter's mask, who threw her
against a vanity and spoke incoherently in her face

before climbing onto the railing
and leaping from the balcony, landing
heavily on the barbecue below,
before racing off on all fours in the slanted morning.

On the radio this afternoon: the police
are looking for an injured man named
Ricardo Villalobos.

The wolves in this county are not to be believed,
and I wonder if they haven't gone too far this time.

PUNISHMENT VIA 14-MINUTE FRENCH FILM

Fuck you, Ricardo Balducci.
Your beautiful film traumatized
a generation of students at King Edward
Public School through the 1980s.

Your story of a lad whose beloved dog
goes missing in Montmartre makes *Le Ballon Rouge*
screen like a delightful romp through old-school Europe.

And though you had no control over Miss C.,
the music teacher sadist who reduced classes to tears
with annual, unannounced screenings of *Clown*—
fuck you.

I've scoured video stores, libraries, pawn shops
to satisfy my morbid curiosity.

But just as I don't need to know
what we'd done as school children to deserve
such scars, I don't need to rewatch your 14 minutes
of agonizing loss and searching
to remember:

the final scene down the blazing cobblestones,
after you've gutted us over and over
on the street corner—

we're now as blinded as the blind man
who, though sad in his own right,
can somehow not escape some cheap masque
of villainy.

Maybe (you foreign bastard) you can take some pride
in your film generating a conditioned response
across the primary grades:

we all knew what was coming
when we saw the projector on its wheeled stand—

your manipulative paean to the milk of human kindness—
and one such day, I simply took off running

convinced our Lakeland, Duffy, would be missing
or dead when I reached home, instead finding
her sleeping fuzzily on her blanket,

staggering up, perplexed but wagging at my early arrival,
perhaps sensing *Clown* had been wheeled out
to scald our cheeks with tears,

to help us better appreciate the brutality of the heart
and the glorious disappointments to come,
through Eddie Vartan's score.

THE LAST NEST

The bell rang as if
      a grackle's head were being
pulverized inside,

though ringing could still
      be heard from the school's far side
beneath the blunt clack,

like there were two bells:
      one clapper wearing its coat
of steel; the other

wearing its coat of
      feathers and blood and the lost
smaller lives of mites.

BELMONT 7's

Me, the guitar player, and the drummer.
We've been recruited as secret detectives.
The office is an old loft, assembled
from disabused sets from *The Fountainhead.*
It's one of those late summer days that remind me
of early fall, of waking up to my worst fears
coming true in another town.
We wear the clothes our fathers wore
when we were born:
golden corduroy sports coats, earth tone
turtlenecks, retarded tartan flammable pants;
we wear moustaches, sideburns, slacks.
Heat is packed in leather rigging.
The gunmetal-blue gun I select from the arsenal
in the wooden drawer will cut a man in half
at one hundred feet.
All part of the agent's retinue,
says the boss, drawing out the syringe.
Soon enough, we will be blasting our way
through a labyrinthine warehouse,
but first we need the shot.
"What's in the needle?" we ask.
"Nothing except the thing that will protect you
from the negative effects of cigarettes," he says.
I offer my arm.
I am at a store buying a pack of cigarettes.
They are called Belmont 7's.
I will need them.
This job is going to be stressful.

UNCLE: FORSAKEN

At the concert

— there was wild hair
    like the musicals once set in February.
The night harem drove through,

        their songs rang in the cribs
of babies. Across the park
        an uncle cried out loud.

He was suffering. His fountain was kaput,
        and he said he'd never write music again,
so help him Satan's hands.

        Why had music forsaken him?
What horror had he forced on these slaves
        that they wished him never to have been born?

Wait. There in the water—
        is that his favourite hat?

PRAYING MANTIS BAKE SALE

What is the weirdest thing, they ask.
Honey is the weirdest thing.
Who decided we were going to eat honey,
saw it dripping hexagonal viscous golden,
and said: We shall eat that which the bees made?
Who was that maniac who said, Let's consume
what the insects make; let's spread their incubation
medium on our toast; put it in pots for kings
in their tombs; withhold it from babies,
for it is a deadly poison? Comb the fields in late summer
alert for the baked goods of the praying mantis.
They are silky good, and oh so tempting
that time of year.

KIOSK

The baby coughed up a key.
It had been missing for some time,
from somewhere.

The man took the key, still wet and
slick as insides,
and tried it all over the house:

nothing. He carried it with him and tried it at post offices,
banks, train stations, storage units—

maybe there was a time machine, grow operation,
or cache of Rococo masterpieces
awaiting liberation—

but the key fit none of these.

Upon arriving home, he tried it on
the neighbours' side door, and it worked.

Man, this baby was going to be fun to have around.

WHOSE CHURCH IS THAT OF THE CERAMIC BULL?

Whose church is that of the ceramic bull
that carved out a place in the furrows

of my baby-smooth brow, baptizing
        me in hot baby blood in the regrettable

toreador motif of young, middle-class Ontario?

The same sacred space where the rug is rolled aside,
so the adults can slash it to ribbons
when the babysitter's cut loose,

and I'm supposed to be asleep in the waterbed,
but instead, lie awake,

fingering the vertical slit
        of the chakra carved into my head,

trying to calm it,
        stop it from calling out

from its laced football mouth
        for the horn of the bull that did it.

*

And it aches today—
the locus of my initiation into the cosmography

of pain beyond the pulsating alien
        of the mothership placenta,

the symptomatic trephination—
        as we stand here smiling by this bowl

of oceans, silage
      sprung from stork bite and fontanelles

in the near-mirror-smooth armour
of the happy ending.

BEACH GLASS

You'd think all the ships of the great glass fleet
had run afoul of a shoal of like-new bb's,

dead-reckoning off your breakwall beach
on the same night, in the same placidity.

And somehow, the payloads all wash up here
with occasional mother sturgeons eyeless in their menses;

advancing legion sharps mellowing with each nuance of the lake floor,
then retreating: a glittering mass of smashed vessels,
rumoured to stave off lymphomas

if kept in a goblet above the kitchen sink, covered in tap water
to remind them of where they used to be

white, brown, green, and blue
and if broken can draw blood, cut anew.

SWARM OF JELLY

Glass only exit bottle
        pineapple of deadly fruit-

shaped swarms of jelly:
        of wasps and mosquitos

        and moths—the worst gift wedding
we ever got, in orange juice.

The funnel they can't find.
        The rough viscous we can't

        transcend. And again our heads
beat our wings.

OBEDIENCE

The soundtrack to our evening
is the police scanner wave action
of the lake, squelching on the beach
as I beat your dog in a corner
of the leather couch, pounding it
the way you pounded Bushmills,
the only defense she has being
your ignorance.

There will come a day when the waves,
the falls, and eventually the sun
will conspire to erode this beach
and erase this home from its brief
honeymoon capitalism.

ERIE LAKE

The separation between the lake
and the air so white

that it looks like the world ends
at the lawn furniture.

Later, stars will rise
from that black enamelled abyss,

backlighting the slats of the deck chairs,
wishing you had a camera

to arrest the night like sperm
smeared on black velvet, flashing purple

and blue. There is smoke, and sparks.

Laughter over there through the trees.

HAIKU

Dopplering gibbous. Cricket
moon.

Sweetgrass and loosestrife
alive in the night

ditches. There's a denuded
tree where a murder

of crows meet.
Or are they turkey vultures?

This poem will not decide.

We're approaching
the Little White Church,

next to the light towers
they call the Five Sisters.

I'm getting tired of this
drive. Even on the coolest

of July nights,
there's heat lightning.

It's like there's a war
over there in the air,

cannons going off
over the lake

like the great yellow
perch battles you read about,

scratched in the beach sand.

TROMPE L'OEIL

Given the choice of what to watch, this Mamet film
or the room and me reflected
in the television screen, I chose *Spartan*.

But there is a part, just before the special-ops rookie gets shot,
where we learn about barometric pressure, rising
and falling, its effect on things in the distance—

objects in the barometry are never where they appear—

and I'm reminded how I tried to explain to my son
why on some days Detroit appears further away from our sun-porch
than on others, and was at a loss.

When the Renaissance Center looms thick and indistinct around the edges
the pressure is low, the air is wet, the molecules
like ocular tapioca, condensing the depth of field.

When the Renaissance Center sits far back, lean and precise,
the pressure is high, the air is dry, the molecules are
like uncooked grain, calling for a new F-stop.

I don't tell him this building is my mineshaft canary,
an exterior mirror reflecting back my looking-glass fears.

So, as the film rolls by in a light-through viewing experience,
I realize I can regrind the jellied lens of my eye by thought
and view the overlaid living room, me slumped half-naked
in front of the couch, lamps burning orange and cinematic.

A variance of molecules exists between me and the TV
that I can bend to my will.

Someone tried to capture this in posters,
but all they could think to do was populate them with dolphins,
dinosaurs, and downhill skiers, and call it magic eye.

THE BAYOU ARMADA

We wondered about the marketability of a book
about a modern-day Noah who shepherds

the dead out of New Orleans on a flotilla of small arks
when the meniscus ruptures and the storm surge climbs the levees

like a tentacled thing of Acadian balladry. A galaxy, spilling into the parish
like a custodial sink left running during a tornado drill.

He reads coffee stains in china cups,
in the wine cellar of Brennan's, where he is the steward.

A man in scuba gear swims up to a window, looks in, sees him
consulting the marks on the enamel, and moves on.

The wineglasses lined up on the stone window ledges float
and topple to the cellar floor. The driest things here are the damsel

flies and wasps that whisper in the shards as the water begins to slide in
slowly, all at once. Every street-level window
giving up the ghost in unison.

He'd watched *Easy Rider* many times in Montreal. He always hated
the interminable scene in the New Orleans graveyard.

He always hated that scene because of this moment:

when the waters come in, he swims his way up the dumbwaiter,
breaking the tension in the deserted dining room,
breast-stroking efficiently through

a field of piqued linen napkins, burgundy beacons
looking for tables. Chandeliers dip baubles in the Gulf.
He will step from a second-storey window

into the new French Quarter—
the South having risen, at least twenty-eight feet above sea level—

and swim for the warehouse where they store the canoes,
lash them together in phalanx and legion and gather the bodies
reconstituting in the warm city seas.

The blacks hail him from the curved parking lot of the Superdome roof.

They become like reindeer afraid to swim. He teaches them and they call
him Coach.

Two weeks later, with shoulders like mountain ranges, they swim
into the mouth of the Ohio Valley.

The papers say it must've been like watching the Spanish fleet
sail in to meet Nelson, if the Spanish fleet were manned by the dead
air-drying in their finery, or something like that.

IF NOT NOW

There are days when I will not be satisfied with
what I've been given, and outward reality—
the dramas of the day that if collapsed would fit,
along with Manhattan, inside this box of Blue Bird
safety matches that have failed to light the barbecue again—
seems even more spacious and filled with mystery
than the most prosaic steel girder. The kind science
tells us is less not there than not not there,
like Tom Dilworth, who in a lecture on Hopkins, Pound,
or possibly Swinburne, threw himself into the lecture hall
wall in an attempt to demonstrate that one day his particles
would array themselves in just such a way as to meet up
perfectly with the spaces between the particles in the cinder
block, and he would simply vanish from sight
and come walking in the classroom door from the
hallway without. He knocked himself out cold.
That it doesn't happen every time is the reason
there's a strike zone, a ground zero, a blank page;
a guitar in the corner, coffee in a chipped porcelain cup,
insults hurled in your direction making love with
your tympanum—the reason some days are too much
with us, lashing each other with the track and field
tape measure you stole from school,
trying to measure up a corner of the yard for some shade
I brought you for Mother's Day (the swirling electrons of
said structure swirling away in the grass against the
back of the house). This day, solid in its domesticity
with trips to Home Depot and Toys "R" Us, is being revealed
to be much less a day than it is a dot pattern,
each dot arrayed just so—I half expect Tom Dilworth
to come tumbling from the hyacinth and tell us
to look each other in the eye, and see the darkling thrushes
of our love there, see the perverse streaks that fail us,
that prevent us from passing through the present moment

and its incumbent troubles, to see that infinitely beyond
the material, there is an intelligence that lines up matter
so we stick in place, not passing through all the time—
charging through rose bushes and coming up in a
smoked meat—that things originate out of something,
mean a lot, and proceed to exactly where
they're supposed to be.

Flicker Rate

FLICKER RATE

In fall do you ever see the leaves
steadily raining to the lawn
and gutters?

More the occasional lazy one, undoing
itself and the air in papery
curves, landing with clicks

but not the steady ochre airburst
of a thousand gifts being unwrapped.
But the evidence is there to be cursed

and sent off to the municipal
mulch heap with raw hands

knowing the stems must let go together
like lovers under the velvet cape
of darkness, like thieves.

Who hasn't considered,
splashing in the shallows, the wave
that pushes them further into the shingle?

Its origins remain as mysterious
as the next, echoes from the unknown prows
of pleasure craft and slave ship

concentric in the grand scheme of things
and moving across the face of the lake
untethered to whatever wind once

kept pace above,
whatever oar struck the time
signature with a slow rococo scrape.

Those who have been in the places
where the wind dies down,
who've seen it toying

with the flowers in the clearing
like they were toy flowers
in a replica clearing;

watched it cease at a private
meridian, without so much as
a memory of a breeze

reaching them where they stand,
lonely,

just feet from where it lipped out
of existence

with no high-water mark,
no flashpoint in the sweetgrass;

those who know the wind
changes tongues and keeps happening,

reinventing itself as a cause,
an invisible mould around a shape,
a feeling, a reason why

afternoon vigils moving incrementally
into evening will not show its hand.

It happens with a rhythm
timed to a flicker rate we're
hardwired to miss:

it allows wasps to build
their stop-frame nests, and peonies
to burst overnight;

children to grow up and
leave you standing there on the carpet,

wondering if you gave them
the order to take flight.

POGROM

We have tried to explain it all away,
succeeding only in talking ourselves
into open-ended corners,

discovering new ways to second-guess
everything and ourselves
back down the highway

to where the absence at home
begins to make more sense
than the absence in the hospital bed.

Were her fevers like a fire
that burned earthly desires away
like possessions after a breakup,

a pre-emptive pogrom,
the pyre of this vale of tears?

Yes, and it stokes your pain.

EXILE

When world leaders languish
in hospital beds
they are often said to be "clinging to life."

But it is a misnomer
to characterize the deathbed
as the lone locus of so much clinging

as it would make it seem
we are all not
always clinging to life,

as if those of us sitting at the end of a dock
with the sports section by a cold lake
are somehow draped across it;

the woman bagging my groceries
is maybe just placed absently on it,
like a banana on an electronic scale.

But we sink our jaws in, immune
to the dog-whistle pitch of its ferocity,
and cling, hardwired oblivious.

What happens on the deathbed
is the agent comes in from the cold exile
dragging behind him the rigging of the wires,

allowing flagging despots and
sainted relations alike
to see that they have always clung to life

the way a child clings to a bear at night,
a soft blessing with fierce jaws.

VESSEL

All the hope in the world depends on half a spoonful
of hospital-grade ice cream.
It is a sign as blazingly clear as anything
lit on fire in the mountains.
Like a wheelbarrow,
like plums that will always be there,
constant, perishable vessels.

SOMETHING OTHER THAN ALABASTER OR MARBLE

So when my uncle, standing at the foot
of the hospital bed, touches and notices
the utter smoothness of my mother's feet
in death

—like she'd never stood on earth
or linoleum; never
chased us down barefoot sidewalks,
spent entire summers without shoes,
had always and forever floated
halfway points off the surface, just close enough

to fool us all;

her one trick toe, bent since childhood
over its neighbour and flattened,
instep, heel, arch, everything
unscathed by this world—

we are meant to find the larger message
alive in the flesh, like the sculpture
in the monolith:

Although we are holding her mouth closed
with a rolled-up towel and a virus
has ravaged her body beyond recognition,
her fifty-eight-year-old feet have no friction

and something other than alabaster or marble
will have to be used to describe them,

and that substance doesn't exist other than as
my mother's perfect feet in death.

LAST THINGS

All the things I did that day
suddenly have this new finality.

Like the man whose kitchen
I sat in, taking notes on his Halloween
light show for the Wednesday paper.
He is the person I was likely talking to
when your condition changed.

Even contained within that October day,
the list of last things could grow infinite;
outside of that day, it would encompass
the breadth of experience—

thirty-two years of last skiing trips, summer cottages,
breast-feedings, diaper-changings,
story-reading, injury-kissing, amend-making,
and my realizing there is about to be
a deluge of first things—

yet I cannot shake myself loose of the last:

eastbound on Riverside Drive—where I likely was
at the time of your death? The last drive home
before Mom died.

The previous Friday's sushi? The last sushi lunch
before Mom died.

Taking photos of children
having their school portraits taken? Undoubtedly my last assignment
before Mom died.

Spark Troop No. 51, who toured the
newspaper offices that afternoon?
Suddenly, they are heretofore and forever
connected to your last day on earth—
the last Spark Troop I saw before
the phone rang.

The phone rang while I was down
on the living room floor, prodding
under the piano with an aluminum
broom handle for a lost action figure,
dragging her out until her feet protruded
from beneath the edge of the soundboard,
like the Wicked Witch of the East's,

my son crying "You found her, you found her!"
as the phone rings in the kitchen—
shattering the simple uncertainty of those last few seconds
of blissful ignorance, known forevermore as
those final seconds before I knew you were gone—

and my son holds up the small lost woman,
and says he won't let her be lost ever again,

and things start happening for the first time.

NATIONAL GEOGRAPHIC

The outfit you wore to our wedding points a Kalashnikov
at a photographer. The knit sweater you wore

to the church picnic in '86 balances bananas on a wicker
trivet in a feverish slum. A denim skirt I have no specific memory of

bulges unexpectedly around a cipher learning to read in a blasted-
out schoolhouse somewhere sickening and hopeful, like the port

the container ship will manoeuvre into, weeks after we've gone through
your closet and drawers and I've renewed my lapsed subscription.

And where other subscribers and newsstand perusers see
warlords' wives gunboating in Yves Saint Laurent at a stronghold

outside Port Loko; some sloe-eyed sapling curved around a desk
in Malanje, dressed for a square dance at the missionary church;

or a fruit-bearing matriarch in Tabi International
cruising the ghettos of Pointe-Noire,

they see the coordinate results of charity, while all I manage to see
are the disembodied clothes, as familiar to me as your rhythm

and the sound of you working in the Iroquois kitchen; a purse
in the crook of your arm from the far end of the mall;
the polished wood of your voice in song....

It's one of these mismatched ensembles I find shackled to a bench
in the back of a DeBeers truck, having been discovered where the dunes

approach the ocean south of Walvis Bay, picking diamonds from the sand
ahead of the vacuums, or so the cutline tells me.

UMBILICAL

I miss you the most at a scar that, undone,
would leave me out of my skin,
naked and raw as I feel.

I was attached here, then clamped off and rotted clean
(some dried fruit in the reliquary of a dresser drawer).
What's left is an injury, an invisible line.

I can plug it into the soil around the sapling red oak
where your memory is intended to live, and hope
it feeds off the nutrients of your ashes.

I can close my eyes and stand there just past the gates
of the park and pretend they are the gates to
a great amusement,

that the sensation I feel at the bottom in my guts,
the agonizing tickle of the Falling Star,
is a laughing communion with you.

WORRY

You are running southbound
down the sidewalk,

and for a split second
disappear behind a tree between us,

and for that split second
you are not in this world

and I am numb with sadness.
And even when you emerge

from the limn of bark and round
the path to the porch

and me, I am struck by
what it was like

for that split second.
The one where you were not.

II

FROSTY

—which is a miracle seeing as how I was born with a clubbed foot,
       missing the fact that I either have to be standing at a stop
or hailing, sometimes walking backwards to kill the boredom.
       Whatever you do, find a different way.

       I love the myth of Sisyphus—it relaxes me like nothing else.
How wonderful it is not to be seeing these same things somewhere else.
       I'm not going to try and convince you with the foliage,
but this is like taking a less travelled path in a yellow wood.

They've notified the press.
       Now the clergy is involved. And a sexton.
I'll say it again:
       and this hill means nothing to me now—

FOG LIKE A PRETTY GIRL'S BANGS

Tell me about those late-winter springs where
the texture and heft of a paper cup
made you nostalgic for mouldy dime-store novels.

A fog like a pretty girl's bangs
rolled up the river from the west—
a tongue of smoke; a ghost recon unit
disguised as a glacier.

Invertebrate, it moved in taffy-pulls,
absorbing its slacked, ropey self all over
the place, and in those places,
became increasingly corpuscular, pancreatic.

Detroit was reduced to a set of bookmatched buildings,
and lightnings arced like ibexes through a tall grass
prairie in the clouds—

and as I stood there with my camera,
I welcomed the advent of the outstretched hand
of a pulp-novel cover girl with eyes like deep lakes

offering transport into the sun-lifted shroud.

DIAMOND-TIPPED AORTAS

Saw blades hanging together make hearts,
so it's always Valentine's Day in the mill

at night,

or a place name that soaks your pant legs
like a distant range of mountains
at the knees

as you set out in the honey of the morning.
Or you set out in the gloaming

with the bug chatter,
the dense blazing star and colicroot.

When you play with your paper dolls,
do you make the sounds of the gun?

Do we die there,
with your flowers,
and your crepe-paper-heart box?

HOTEL EMPIRICAL

It was the high-water mark of the season.
I rescued a cheetah from a castle
without so much as a minute's worth of training,
a victim of happenstance's delightful nightmare. Someone said:
"That wasn't a cheetah, that was some kind of gelatin."
Once they had removed my fist from the vicinity of their life,
I took them to the basement, showed them the castle,
and said, "Does that look like horse's hooves to you?"
They had to admit it did not,
and we agreed they should remain there, chained
to the drainpipe, until further notice.

LEVELLER

I was reading about a man receiving a sign
in the form of a blazing
ash tree outside his window.
Within minutes, it was nothing but an
artery of sticks where yellow used to be,
and the man was at a loss,
unexpectedly affected by the autumn.
When I looked up from reading,
it was snowing, and I was reminded
of the end of "The Dead" where the snow is falling
so faintly, so equally, and just
as the wind denudes burning fall trees,
a merciful, magician's prop of a blanket comes—
ecclesiastical-white and killing
without regret, without judgment—
and preserves under its shroud
the myriad small mysteries of the altars of change,
preserving them in such a way
that had I not looked outside at all that day,
He still would've found a way to show me
—a buildup of frost in the freezer;
the Fibonacci spiral in a teacup.

LOAD

His money shot goes on forever.
It didn't just coalesce in the supposed
fall, then fall impotent. It didn't gel
into us and things and rabbits and then
dry and flake off his mouse, or run down
the inside of nothing's leg. We are in it

now, here,
in this suburban parking lot,
at this café table, with these oversized
mugs amidst this flurry of poplar that snows
in disjointed strings like cum in a hot tub.

White aimless stars have a destination
we understand but can't divine. Their swarm
in flight what happens in our throes, the rivers
that flow from us, in emulation, to scale.

BEACH GLASS II

We lower the earthmovers to the beach by hand.
Rebuilding this section below the rustic breakwall
could take the better part of the hour.

We are like Christos. You rename us Dan and Steve—
our rolling stock is yellow, our resolve to sculpt
the beachhead as pure as lightning.

This beach never ceases to yield a glassblower's epididymis
of exploded vessels. Small thermal treasures.

And I've checked the local archives and
no lumbering ship of the glass fleet
is known to have run into trouble off the fierce

Wigle Creek current, over the phantom depth of the
Colchester South trench. Still, the ship inches
along the bottom, a scouring brisket that one day

will leap from the lip at the end of the lake, sailing in
gothic regalia into the conversation of honeymooners

who comment on the merchant fleet of the glass trade,
the new Ontario gem economy.

And back on this ribbon of sand we build
a small, hot town—

where streets curve and undulate through Usonian
neighbourhoods, and husbands and wives in miniature

mine blue, green, and the occasional
motherlode of singular orange from the shingle

for the glimmering glass windows that block
their Turkel House walls, unaware of ghost ships at Niagara Falls,
not knowing we've carved them out a place for jealousy

with toys; where men practice the essentials of the knife fight
in the streets, their invisible blood running down the gutters,

the ambergris of some future hunt.

And if lightning struck now, would the sand turn to glass,
the glass to sand?

Have we messed with the beachhead,
like the cities of the plain?

FLAGS OF BURGEONING NATIONS

The genius behind the flags of burgeoning nations
is that they are mistakes:
each of the four slightly different
than the one preceding;
each a square of mallard purple
stitched with the invisible threads of hope
onto a field of Astroturf green;
each birthed from the printer near my desk
like an ideology on twenty-pound stock,
the heritage and language
children salute to in the mornings,
the past and future of some multitude lost in time
when days were lopped from calendars
in an effort to distance one's blood and tongue
from Avignon or Rome.

That time, rather than be left a ribbonous rush
on the cutting-room floor of our mythmaking,
was placed somewhere,
in order to be disprovable and scientific.
Select hit men, thieves, and maiden aunts were sent
to colonize the time,
and keep it, because not unlike matter—
time cannot be created or destroyed,
only banished like a mercenary
who, once the contract is carried out,
is judged too knowledgeable to keep around,
too dangerous to imprison,
too charming to execute and impossible
to dispose of, regardless.

Who can say why it's taken so long
for them to decide on a national standard,
other than that time moves differently for them,

whether they rake perpetual leaves
in those ten October days
excised from the calendar by papal bull in 1582,
or simply hold place in the kalends, ides, and nones
of the ninety vapid days
inserted as a corrective by Caesar back in 45 BC,
or reside in any other microcosm of dates
secreted to a backwater
in a lacklustre attempt
to get Easter to fall on the same day each year.
And who's to say why their flags
are not more in keeping with their culture—
a singular spectral field, embossed in wraiths of white.

Instead, identical purple squares
anchored crookedly in the top left quadrant
of identical green rectangles.
And why were these flags unfurled from a printer
here at this day job,
itself a placeholder past gestation,
and who hit print to queue them up?
No one from the small staff
ever came to claim responsibility,
to claim the young flags as their own,
ex post facto or by proxy.

So, I pause to tape them
into the final four pages of a notebook,
an annex for these paper tapestries
like the treasures of Bohemia and Imperial Russia
whisked away to safety
in the face of an advancing army,
the vanguard on the threshold's museum.

LOCUSTS, NOT WORDS

for Lee Ranaldo

When the sheets are snapped from the furniture
and their whiteness gives up the surface as they break
like chiselled marble curtains, light as wraiths,

they'll return to the black ones you placed over your things,
when you locked the door and just left,

implored to do so by the first poem in a collection,
the phone left off the hook
in a movie that never ends.

Those words that devour those fields are only words.
Right your house and clear away the wreckage of the past,
and you won't fear the swarming plague.

Re-entering, you'll remove the sheets
and find what remains is a place of things
falling apart by design;

where form, substance, and force were never wanting.
Where even the locusts fulfill a role, in this,
the longest movie any of us has ever been in.

ON THE REOPENING OF THE BOOK CADILLAC,
DETROIT, MICHIGAN, NOVEMBER 2008

We have no cool hotels in this town.
But we have nostalgia:
the place where memory gathers
around an old wound, rallying it to language

about places with pancake houses,
and a place that burned to the river—

but we have no cool hotels here.
Attempts to mythologize the Viscount
are onanistic to the point of indecency.
The majorette on the sign at the Diane

Motor Inn hasn't put her foot down
in decades, and no one's been interviewed
on her roof; she's never been the city of eclectic refuge;
you would beg her beds' secrets

to be gone by morning.
Revolutions don't die between the sheets
of the Ivy Rose; movements aren't born
in the bathtub at the Welcome Travelers;

no one's ever been shot in the lobby
of the Airport, because the Airport doesn't
have a lobby, not even a courtyard.

It's the office or gravel parking lot for you.
Take your pick.

ANTLERS OF MAPLE

Thanks for the rhododendrons. When they explode arterial over the porch
railing, Pantone 2582, they allow me to cast aside the false,
shallow soil of you.

VCRs, Persian and Oriental rugs with black lung—we've been too nice
to decline, too afraid to stack it Tuesdays
in the dew-beaded alley wildflowers.

Sneaking it out like hot merchandise, under cover of butterscotch
schnapps, praying sheeny men claim it in the night
and disappear it to the many mansions of the meek.

Thanks for these brilliant blasts, roots lost in a spidery pyroclast.
Don't stop complaining about soil acidity
when you expel them to the sidewalk

between the houses. When a branch from our tree fell into your garden
in an autumn afternoon windstorm, I found the branch dragged back to
us, over your wrought-iron

fence. And I wore it like 147-point antlers to your Halloween party—
a stroke of dry whimsy, I walked in sideways
and it took me three minutes, still coming

up the stairs and heading out the back door while standing at the cocktail
crustaceans, impressing the fuck out of your new coterie of
bottom-of-the-barrel coxswains.

We paid for the minister at your media-circus wedding.
Thanks for the rhododendrons. Oh, yeah: and the waffle iron.

CECI N'EST PAS UNE STAGMOMANTIS CAROLINA

It was juvenilia and way too long
and in shortening it, we ended up here,
in this Montreal tobacconist (his shoppe, not him).
The kind of place that should be selling cuckoo
clocks, only it deals in a universe of pipes
with all the charm of a Sears-Roebuck
credit department. The pipe I want keeps moving,
relocating like a praying mantis among other stick
insects, keeps clicking into locks, popping out of Swiss chalets,
oscillating Cavendish and chicory, riding the waxing and waning
pine cones of time in a glockenspiel-
and-hammer dulcimer-less interregnum—
and it becomes apparent in the anticipatory silence
of dumbwaiter chains that we've been running out of time
from the very beginning, and in an unprecedented flourish of éclat
and élan I produce a leather pipe case—
there must be a French name for these, like *peloquin*, or
pletruquard—and place it open on the glass countertop,
and when we open our eyes one has crawled into the
crushed velvet mould and sleeps there
like a small boy of polished oriental wood.
We watch him sleep. The birds erupt, but nothing
wakes him. We're not even sure it's a boy. In fact, I'm
the only one here now. It's just me and the tobacconist,
who places a walking stick in his mouth and lights it,
stoking its caldera with the bellows of his kisses.
Ropey strings are loosed on the room as we stand and
watch as it sleeps, a small soothsayer,
whose head and torso stain the sheets.

GHOSTS OF THE PICNIC

How wonderful it would be,
you think, to have a horse to visit
in a stall in the woods—
a magi to sit and coalesce with, throwing prudence
away like a duplicate hockey card,

untying a knotted blanket you once used to capture
memories at a picnic
and left in the wheel well of the Volvo:

sandwich ghosts,
with the bones of grapes.

You never understood the schwa sound,
and you don't understand this.

L-TRYPTOPHAN

(It's kicking in, no? A log splits and sparks
throw themselves against the linked mercy
of the grate,

      slumbering to waving paper on the hearthstones.)

They found them packed with explosions,
atom-heart cells, the ones who preferred to be oils
over fossils had a better chance of becoming cars:
lightning kissed beaches, melted trees.

(Rising back to the room, a fire, a football game,
my son in a lightsaber duel.)

A child has written:
a skeleton is something to hitch meat to.
It is what's left after the insides
have been taken out,
and the outsides have been taken off.

(Pie? Yes, and coffee. Everyone's working
on a crossword, or plans for a hostile takeover
of the lake—

      the lines further blurred by an apneatic's
        ruptured bathysphere.)

If the globe is bisected like a halved orange
by a lion running around the world forever,

and if we've been deceived that parasitic larvae
enter our world through our feet—
a semantic gaffe of the highest order—

then sell this stuff in the laneways
beside neighbourhood grocers;
streak the chin with the grease of the goose.

(New watch. A copy of the latest *Harper's*. My first
sports coat.)

Drag anything five hundred feet in a second and you're
a collapsing dark matter, in my book.

STRANGELET

Dark matter, dark days,
and the dark ring of the supercollider,
fired up in August's slumber.

A little black hole
gone rogue—
on the lam on the lawn—swirling
around in the hostas, the town,

sucking our canvas
like a little gyre in the bath.

When crossing the border
into and out of France
90,000 times per second

grew so quickly tiresome,
Swiss strangelet,

there is too much of you
in such a small non-package.

IGNEOUS CONDUIT

Unruly rocks,
wild in their slow predictability,
keep surfacing.

Farmers build quaint walls from them—
we drive by in praise, only the writer back-thinking
the harrow scars, the bleeding knuckles, a condescension
of leaves settling down before the wall—
but we are not here to heap praise
upon these would-be husbands of dirt.

Thanks for the food, but you are fools.
You and the International Harvester cannot beat the rocks
that rise, continue to rise, will always rise,
to the subcutaneous mystery
out there through the kitchen window. Out there

where now there is snow, or pestilence, or dirt bikes.
Where God has seen your worst defeats,

where in the spring you will nearly set the dirt ablaze,
drawing the blade over that much mineral.
Fieldstones the size and shape of your stomach
where last year you pulled its quartzy cousin,
this feldspar-flecked gastropod, eating your lunch.

Praise instead the thermal convection current:
core magma, through mantle, asthenosphere, and crust,
an igneous conduit to here, born on fire,
older than the principles used to date them
by the time they arrive grey and cold
and out-of-control in their unwavering rhythm underground.

A wall is not a significant enough monument
even if it extends to the woodlot in the back.

Continue the conduit up, markers to the path
of least resistance, aerials to futility,
towers towards the half-life.

AKOUSMATA

She stirred the fire with a dagger against
things whispered in her ear. He spat with disgust
on his hair cuttings and nail clippings,
trimming the lamp next to the mirror
in the dark. Neither spoke.
Without a word for gravity, it could not be
described. They described without speaking
a framework where several men lift a rock
while one man undoes their work.
The parklife around them bristled with
generation: heads like adzes that carve
the wooded air; paws the terminals of ragged genital
arches against the night. They've been counselled
not to eat beginning nor end, nor that
from which first development
unfurls—
a moon-white legume's arm curling out
into the forest floor
amongst testicular droppings,
truffles, and spores. The whisperings are about
what's signified, what is, and what should be
refrained from, received without discussion,
and preserved. And if "hours can be consumed
by hatpin issues alone," then whatever they
are doing out here, quietly
imperilled in the night,
is good, because they are not at rest,
and have counselled nothing
to each other that is not
what is best for the counselled,
for these ninety-six things received in the ear
are holy.

THE ICE-CREAM HOUR

You trust me the way only a new acquaintance can,
and when you return I've been making cones
several times too large, destroying your profit margins,

like you had ice cream to burn.
Everyone's standing around eating these huge confections.
I had plans to just sit on that bench
and think about a poem, because the air was pregnant
with that when you left with the bouquet.

We're like a movie made about your trust
and projected against the side of this old bait shoppe,

so that when we talk, we talk about death and
faith and curious birds,

and with my neck camera-strap-raw, I begin to suspect
the eagles are our Aloysius Snuffleupagus:
showing up to crash golden talons into the river
for everyone but me.

Or like young Holden's secret goldfish:
guarded like a jealous oracle kept in the bowl

of your influence, wings weighed down
with mountains of pistachio and tigertail.

But the hour of ice cream was upon us
like a whole-milk plague—

something with nuts, an aether of licorice,
me, handy with a scoop, digging through poison
for ribbon veins—

an hour you told me would come,
as you told me bald eagles fished here,

in the perch-choked shallows off the dock,
every day from their aerie on Fighting Island.

NEAR MUTED SWANS

A likeness like an electrocardiogram fire
bleeding a blood orange running
into what can only be called corpse-paint grey,

then rust-wet waterline.
I'm playing this game with the top of the food chain
in the boats docked along the canal,

with a long way to go through a Confederate
town at night while muted swans fill a bend in the river.

THE PANDEMIC OF LONELINESS

Consider heartsickness in vampires:
a possible cause for the migration of the plague.
A sloop slips into port in the morning.
See the fragile chimneysweep running with a coffin
of soil across the vacated squares of the cities
haunted by the stillness of the disappeared.

How have all these people disappeared,
replaced by the flea-ridden familiars of vampires?
Their gift to these ancient cities,
now pockmarked maps of the plague,
the black infested soil of each coffin
rafted down a river, closed to the morning.

Damned barren calm of morning:
the sloop crew unidentifiable, not disappeared.
At the first sign of swollen glands, a man climbs into a coffin
as black as the nightmare blackness of vampires.
Real-estate agents unwitting catalysts of the plague,
their women the oblivious succubi of cities,

the pure-hearted target buried in the cities,
their throats, lips, wrists themselves a plague
on the heartsickness that withers like devils in the morning,
devils that had no intention of being fathers of the disappeared.
Devils who would likely rather be dead than vampires,
shipping themselves towards an industry of coffins,

a self-negating building and fulfilling of coffins
in the dancing vanguard of ghost cities.
There is something pathetic about these vampires.
There is something inevitable about this morning,
after all but those walled in by iconography are disappeared,
it all boils down to a pandemic of loneliness that plagues

Seville, Constantinople, Marseilles—undone by the most common plague.
Cyprian, Justinian, Emmaus—synonymous with a sea of cheap coffins.
But have the undead found lovers, or just disappeared?
Birds, who need no conveyance to travel, now threaten cities.
You may feed them toast in the morning,
their wings not the scalloped leather of the vampire.

Have you considered the vampire heartsickness, the plague
that can fill a coffin, unpopulate the once-subtle morning,
and leave cities devoid of everything but the disappeared?

SHIP BREAKING

Night falls on the beach at Chittagong.
The work continues and the beach becomes an inferno
       of smoke and flames and filth.

Over one hundred ships meet their death here every year—
the beach becomes the mine:
       from luxury liner to lake freighter, the wretched

of the mudflats torch them into steel plates
until there's nothing there to hold up the asbestos
       and poison that builds up the ten miles

of beach where these thirty operations break the vessels,
fighting over the prized bone of the propeller;
       the dark pearl of a commode,

sold along the road that leads to the Bay of Bengal—
a bustling secondary economy for the things
       that will not melt in a blast furnace.

Beaching a ship is a very delicate operation.
A man they call the Executioner
       calculates the movement of the tides,

the swell, the wind, the phase of moon
to the minute, wedging a ship that will be set upon
       by braying barefoot hounds carrying only welders'

tools and chains, raped of every last weld and ghost
the moment it impacts on the hot black mud.
       A delicate operation

for something that started as an accident,
when a cyclone's tidal bore left a giant cargo ship
       stranded on a pristine beach.

FURTHER EXPLORED IN THE PANTOMIMES

Storefronts of ill repute have been liberated
of their stocks of whips. We've learned a horse
does not look out of place in the church;
that the rider is the drapery, the horse the transcendent heart
of this ninety-second reel around the fountain.
But what will this race teach us of covetousness and cruelty;
the appetite for marrow and tendon; the crack
of veterinary sidearm parenthetical
to the starter's pistol; the honour of capturing
a non-denominational tapestry; business acumen?

A father stands in the chapter house
holding a horse by its bridle, a mercenary
in the silks of a superhero embroidered with depictions
of ideals and concepts further explored in the pantomimes
and interpretive dances that grind down
the avenues within baronies redrawn
like a riding. Where standards are unfurled
in the streets by children, the aged, the morbidly
overhyped speaking the litany of Palios past
in gold streamer, Wedgwood blue
under a high-pressure ceiling:

the deeds of riders more adept
at bribery and summer kitchen negotiation
recalled in blood purple the pitch of bruised veal.
They found it standing in their garden three days
before the race, staring blackly at its grand brown reflection
in the pool, as if contemplating a new haircut,
jackknife, cannonball, or something more distressing,

like coming unglued through the final turn
creating a new joint below the forelock,
spilling a rider and ruining dinner—

ruining everything completely.

TORREGAVETA BEACH

O the freshness of the bread.
O the joy spelled out in the teeth marks
on this end of that local cheese we both enjoy so much.

The bluebottle fly trapped in the blue bottle
abandoned to the sand, lured
by the sweet dregs that balance inside.

The fly on the eye of the dead girl,
where she lay in the sand like a vessel,
unmatched at the hip with her sister,

where the wind has blown discarded towels
from their prying, hungry eyes.

I wish we only still knew of their raging feet.
I'm not sure I'll be able to finish

off the sweetmeats.

        But here, with the toy
wooden tombs rumbling on their shoulders,

come the men from the town—

how they all stare and refuse to stare
at us across their judgmental brows;

how we watch them like terns
flirting with the surf.

        Look, one of them has those shoes
I nearly bought in Naples.

THE BEST POSTCARD IN THE WORLD

She dripped like brown and orange fruit.
A talisman pulled from the mouth of a lemon shark.
"I like to pretend I'm light as air," she tells him,
a Willendorf amongst the iodine milkshakes, shameless
in the shallow end in the slanting light pulled over
by the 5:12 out of Ft. Myers, the Gulf air fights to both swallow
and preserve their arched steps—

A slug outside the ladies' cabana spent all afternoon looking for a shell.
It moved with more purpose than anyone else on the island that day,
its progress recorded in a register like the Gulf tides.
Teenagers played shuffleboard on courts laid out
like landing strips in the palm

and sea grape.
Combing the beaches before dawn and the shark patrol,
the telltale veins and rinds of prosciutto and melon on a silver tray,
beach mystery boilerplate informing his empire of frogmen
who execute the slow release of lightning whelk, king's crown, paper fig,
spoors from a bag in a clicking cloud

minutes before the retreat of high tide.
Whispers in the mangroves and Spanish moss carry in the silence
of passing storms and punctuate his laboured progress down the many
steps to his rental car; the occasions he ventures from his condo
as rare as rarest Junonia, a plague drinking the plumage
of some forgotten species.

Vanity-press colophons line up like invertebrate portals on his shelves.
Gaps in the fossil record representing copies lent to the ladies
around the pool whose sons and daughters scour the pages for code

and signal various times, amounts, dates, and figures
with the discs and cues, clothes and posture:
the gentle dead language of the 10 off—

"I like to know I'm as heavy as a teaspoon of sun," he whispers.

STUCK BETWEEN STATIONS

As it turns out, we do have
       your 25-foot orange extension cord,
the dirty colour of orange like a sick person's blood,

that sick person being me—
       sick with analysis when we find it
dormant in the toy room,

like a viper under the rock
       of childhood's sedimentary abandon,

the bizarre deciduous shrub
       of my circulatory system run to rust,
denuded of me, and left standing there stripped

by your expectations before falling
       to the floor in a looping coil

where I grab its end and flick it
       across the room like a bullwhip

to get an idea of its length.
       Mesmerized by its oscillations

I flick it, and flick it again,
       and hear you asking for it

again, and again
your disappointment.

THE HISTORY OF BASEBALL

You are teaching Nathanael how to use the three-in-one
progressive T-ball set we got him for his second birthday.

Almost eleven years since we shared lip balm
and took crystal meth
at the double bill at Vertigo's,
and I never knew you batted left.

"What secrets she keeps from me," I whisper,
watching, rapt.

I've been reading *Actual Air* on a chair in the pool,
but thinking about graphic novels and how I am jealous of them,
how the spatial constraints allow for so much exploration,
so much room to not describe the details.

When I see you standing there in our overgrown yard
demonstrating for our son how this thing works
(he keeps stuffing toy trains and action figures down the barrel of the tee),
it's obvious: we've missed a baker's decade's worth
of grapefruit league in the backyard.

"I feel like I don't even know who you are," I say, rising
slowly, like Cpt. Willard, from the eerily still waters,
robbed of my ignorance, the scales of unknowing peeled
by your practice cut in the cicada drone.

And I make you put the bat down, and instruct you to clear your mind
of all preconceptions about the game, before picking up the bat—
made of the same stuff dolls' arms are made of.
You belong to the tradition of Kirk Gibson and my cousin Glenn,
the only two confirmed lefties I can think of.

Lou Whittaker, too:
he led off every game of the '84 World Series with a single
slapped through the opposite side of the infield.

You lead off (your first at-bat of our marriage)
with a line shot into the raspberries that you and Natty retrieve
using the garden wand. It is a fine hit.

Hours later, I am still in the pool, stricken, and have forsaken the chair
in favour of being up to my neck in the single depth.
You've taken Nathanael inside, and I can hear him playing and you
opening the fridge and padding around barefoot.

But the sustained note beneath it all is
you, and your self-admitted weirdness at the plate.

Although I know you're five-foot-seven, blond, blue, 34B,
a native of Toronto, of the Holy Roman persuasion,
it's like I never bothered to turn your card over
to check your vital stats.
There's a whole world there to be digested, extrapolated, committed
to memory:

these figures—the secret history of your household namehood:
2B, SO, AVG., BB—should be tattooed between your
shoulder blades, in the hollow of your
back, your inner thigh....

Is there any other sinister thing you want to reveal?
Your sore shoulder is not from sleeping
funny, but from burning your arm out throwing curveballs
since convent school? Vaseline under the cap bill? Synthetic cork
in the plastic bat? Pine tar of Aunt Jemima liberally applied?

Regardless, it's bad scouting on my part.

With Nathanael and his unorthodoxy,
holding the bat like a ram,
knocking the ball off the tee like he's playing billiards,
we're only six shy of a roster.

We should have more Sundays like this,
full of the mystery in our swings,
and in the semaphore from third base,
represented by that party hat.

HOUSE BALLOONS

They've been hanging around the house
for eighteen days now,
though the birthday is long over.

I've personally dispatched half a dozen
others, breaking them into primary-coloured
skin in my hands,
but these two have taken up residence.

Wraiths riding unaccounted for
jet streams through our rooms,
their pace creepy, directionless
in their ability to end up in the narrows
of the kitchen, about to wash a glass.

Lolling up next to me as I write,
outsized heads, lozenges of foil—
looking better suited for the depths
of the oceans, flashing things on the verge
of collapse.

Flagella of yellow ribbon
trailing like benign whips.

Yet, they are upstairs, here,
existing at eye level, helium-deprived,
incognito as our son's most beloved
cartoon idols, where an hour ago one was
looking out the front window, the other—
the one we call Arthur—
was wrestling with the cat,
having been attacked at the piano,
picking out some Philip Glass.

You broke the silence last night,
giving words to exactly what I'd been thinking
as we watched the other one sail
up the stairs, after a long day of
learning how to live.

And I just caught them in
flagrante delicto in the sun room—
pulsing around each other like lava in a lamp.

And it makes me wonder—
why us, and how long
will they stay?

ONE FOR JOHN

> *And if this was nearly*
> *all—this and the woodpecker's*
>
> *prospecting—there would be*
> *more to come. For the Lord*
> *went winking to his grave.*
>
> —from "On Good Friday" by John Ditsky

Three days after you died I
took down *scar tissue*

and hoped you'd had a chance to check
the last phone booth you passed

for the coins you coveted, I think,
more for their finding than their worth—

a chance for some small action, reprieve
from some inner dullness, maybe

(but I'm only guessing at what
could be larks, could be basalt plains

within)—your taciturnity,
that poorly disguised laugh of dancing lips

and wet eyes that prohibited you from talking
too much about yourself.

Hence the long silences that people
still talk about, even days after

you've slipped out of the room unnoticed,
again,

to wherever the '46 Tigers play in perpetuity,
and there's always a shiny quarter

in every slot, and the music is played
according to serial number,

the numbers found in the card catalogue
you brought with you

when you winked out of the room,
yet again,

but this time for good.

TWILIGHT CINCINNATI

With baseball on the radio
I could drive forever.
I'd drive right by the house,
slowing only to make sure
the cat had water in her bowl,
and I would drive
straight through the dark
to the Gulf Coast of Florida,
with my hand on your thigh
and the Tigers beating up on the Twins
the entire time.

TENUOUS CITY

You were the threshold of love and desperation,
looking forward to your martyrdom in a moratorium
of narrative

      in the tragic euphoria of no laughter,
and the notes that aren't played,
drawing lots in a morass of carbon monoxide
and repeated gestures.

Slave to the 19th hole. Slave
to the Pavlovian response of rocks
at low tide—
the rocks are your organs:

      toxic and pointilist landscapes.
A module for the wind.
A covenant house.
More trees in a landscape of trees.
Gentle, anxious, and numbing
each straggling piece

      to sleep before evening
as the headlines refresh in the new weather,

and in any dangerous love,
any harmless fantasy,
and the grain of the wood is an impulse

leaving nothing behind but
the tenuous city
of its wandering tracks, that fall
into the wood like night inaudible,

    like a bridge of cold
reception,
and we don't quite know
what to do about it
(and nobody is going to like
        the ending, which is unfortunate)

because we cannot be really naked
in this period of unprecedented frost
and speculation,

and the crushed fruit of all
this brilliant nonsense.

CENTO FOR A RAT-PACKER

Bob Hope, the wisecracking street-corner thug—
       I feel you very close to me.
Moments later, the skipper of the schooner

       ascended and made his entrance
like lavish origami animals returned.
       In her modesty she ordered the cobalt

dragon placed by some expensive chocolate
       like a number after a long,

baffling math equation.
       We were back on our terrace sipping
wine, so there's no confusion

about the experience:

       I took the silence and snapped it.

Notes & Acknowledgements

"I Remember the Way Things Weren't" contains a reference to Richard Linklater's film *Waking Life*.

"The Viscount Hotel" is for Matthew St. Amand.

"Perspectives on the Death of an Amateur Filmmaker" is inspired by the Werner Herzog documentary *Grizzly Man*.

"Sidney Crosby" was inspired by an instant messaging session with Vanessa Baker. The poem is for her.

"Uncle: Forsaken" is a mistranslation from the original Dutch of F. L. Bastet's poem "Een jongen."

"Frosty" is after "The Hill" by Mark Strand.

"Locusts, Not Words" is a response to Lee Ranaldo's poem "Locusts."

"Ghosts of the Picnic" borrows from James Tate's poem "Everything for the Horse."

"Strangelet" is about the Large Hadron Collider, a particle accelerator located 100 metres below the ground outside of Geneva, Switzerland. It was built by the European Organization for Nuclear Research to investigate the fundamental building blocks of the universe. There was some concern it could create a theoretical piece of matter called a strangelet that could potentially devour/catastrophically alter existence.

"Akousmata" was written after encountering the term for the first time in Thomas Pynchon's *Against the Day* and contains a quoted passage from that novel. Akousmata are a list of superstitious rules, tips for hygiene, and bits of advice for daily living originally compiled by Pythagoras (c. 570–c. 480 BC) and practiced literally by the Pythagoreans. There is some historical evidence that the akousmata were cult precepts or passwords.

Examples of akousmata include: "Do not look yourself in the mirror by candlelight," "Be not held by uncontrollable laughter," "Always turn the vinegar cruet away from yourself," and "To die standing firm and receiving wounds on the front of the body is good. The reverse is bad."

"The Ice-Cream Hour" is for Cherie Dillen.

"Near Muted Swans" contains a reference to the traditional song "The Fox Went Out on a Chilly Night."

"The Pandemic of Loneliness" is based on Werner Herzog's *Nosferatu* and is dedicated to Emily Schultz.

"Ship Breaking" borrows from a CBS News online article from November 2006 about ship breaking in India.

"Further Explored in the Pantomimes" was inspired by a June 1988 *National Geographic* article and photographs of the Palio horse race in Siena, Italy.

"Torregaveta Beach" is based on a news story about two young Roma girls who drowned at Torregaveta Beach outside of Naples, Italy. People continued sunbathing and eating within view of their bodies.

"Stuck Between Stations" borrows its title from a terrific song by The Hold Steady. I was encouraged to write this one by my good friend Paul Vermeersch.

"Tenuous City" is after John Ashbery's "The Wave."

"Cento for a Rat-Packer" contains randomly selected lines from the following poets and poems: "The Bob Hope Poem" by Campbell McGrath; "Song" by Charles North; "Manta Ray Jack and the Crew of the Spooner" by Steve Venright; "27,000 Miles" by Albert Goldbarth; "The Daisy. The Dolphin. The Dagger. The Dragon" by Paul Vermeersch; "Sensuous Reader" by Elaine Equi; "After the Storm" by Jason Heroux; "Clouds

Gathering" by Charles Simic; "Natalie Loses Weight" by David McGimpsey; and "Tragedy's Greatest Hits" by James Tate.

Earlier versions of several of these poems appeared in *Blank Magazine, Draft 4.3, Iota, Magma, Monday Night, Nthposition, Poetry Super Highway,* and *This Magazine.* My thanks to the editors of these publications.

The poems "Presenting The Sleep of Dolls," "Torregaveta Beach" and "Wolves" appeared in the pamphlet *Uninvited, Like the Clouds.*

The following people have provided friendship, support, advice, and words of encouragement during the writing of these poems: Matthew St. Amand, Paul A. Toth, Michael Epp, Lucy Powell, Emily Schultz, Todd Swift, Ken Babstock and Sean Grayson. They have helped more than they know.

A special thanks to Paul Vermeersch who looked at a very early version of this manuscript. His guidance and friendship have been invaluable.

My editor Stuart Ross believed in these poems. His guidance, ear, and insightful hand helped shape this collection. For that, I owe him a heart-felt thank you. My thanks also to my publisher Denis De Klerck, and Leigh Nash at Mansfield Press, for making this happen. I am humbled by their attentions and enthusiasm.

Although they did not always agree with my decisions and career choices, my father and my mother (to whom this book is dedicated) gave me everything I have. For them, and for my sister Thea, I am grateful.

My wife, Jennifer, and our children Nathanael, Jonah and Thomasin have lived through the writing of these poems. They have been patient, forgiving, and inspiring—each in their own way—and for that, I love them, and owe them.

Robert Earl Stewart was born in Windsor, Ontario, in 1974. He graduated from the University of Windsor and has an M.A. in English from McGill University. His poetry has appeared in journals in Canada, the U.S., and Great Britain, including *Monday Night, Nthposition, Iota, Magma, Rampike, The Moosehead*  *Anthology X,* and *This Magazine.* He lives in Windsor with his wife, Jennifer, and their three young children. He works for a weekly newspaper and has been working on a novel since 2001.

BOOKS FROM MANSFIELD PRESS

Poetry
Leanne Averbach, *Fever*
Diana Fitzgerald Bryden, *Learning Russian*
Alice Burdick, *Flutter*
Margaret Christakos, *wipe.under.a.love*
Pino Coluccio, *First Comes Love*
Gary Michael Dault, *The Milk of Birds*
Pier Giorgio Di Cicco, *Early Works*
Pier Giorgio Di Cicco, *The Visible World*
Christopher Doda, *Aesthetics Lesson*
Rishma Dunlop, *Metropolis*
Ollivier Dyens, *The Profane Earth*
Suzanne Hancock, *Another Name for Bridge*
Jason Heroux, *Emergency Hallelujah*
Jason Heroux, *Memoirs of an Alias*
Carole Glasser Langille, *Late in a Slow Time*
Jeanette Lynes, *The Aging Cheerleader's Alphabet*
David W. McFadden, *Be Calm, Honey*
Lillian Necakov, *The Bone Broker*
Catherine Owen & Joe Rosenblatt, with Karen Moe, *Dog*
Corrado Paina, *The Alphabet of the Traveler*
Corrado Paina, *Souls in Plain Clothes*
Jim Smith, *Back Off, Assassin! Poems New & Selected*
Robert Earl Stewart, *Something Burned Along the Southern Border*
Steve Venright, *Floors of Enduring Beauty*
Brian Wickers, *Stations of the Lost*

Fiction
Kent Nussey, *A Love Supreme*
Kent Nussey, ed., *Particle & Wave*
Tom Walmsley, *Dog Eat Rat*

Non-fiction
Pier Giorgio Di Cicco, *Municipal Mind*
Amy Lavender Harris, *Imagining Toronto*